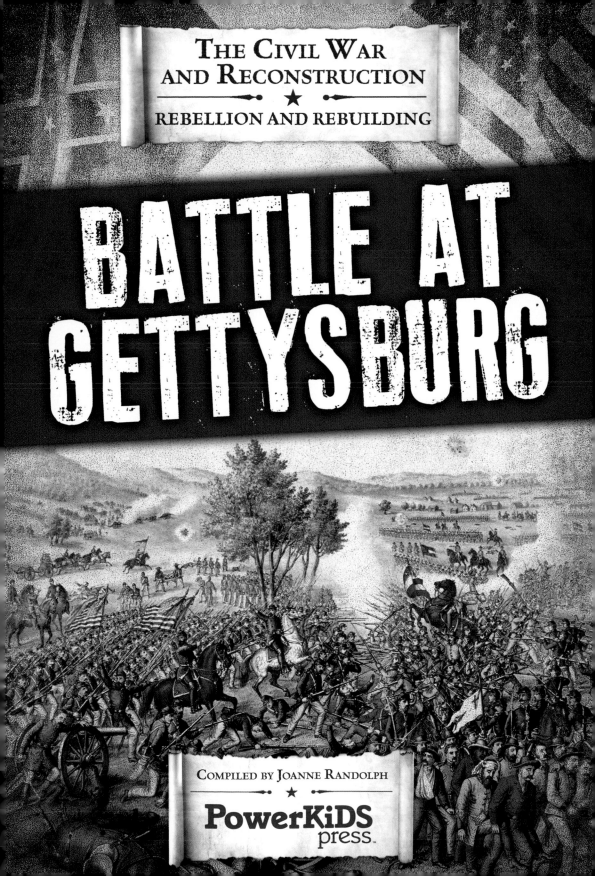

THE CIVIL WAR AND RECONSTRUCTION
★
REBELLION AND REBUILDING

BATTLE AT GETTYSBURG

COMPILED BY JOANNE RANDOLPH
★

PowerKiDS
press™

Published in 2018 by The Rosen Publishing Group, Inc.
29 East 21st Street, New York, NY 10010

"Gettysburg and the Civil War" by Harold Holzer and Mark Clemens from Cobblestone
Magazine (May 2010)
"Gettysburg: From Farmland to Battlefield" by Caryl Simon-Katler from Cobblestone
Magazine (July 1998)
"Lost at Gettysburg" by Rollie Aden from Cobblestone Magazine (July 1998)

Cataloging-in-Publication Data

Names: Randolph, Joanne.
Title: Battle at Gettysburg / compiled by Joanne Randolph.
Description: New York : PowerKids Press, 2018. | Series: The Civil War and Reconstruction:
rebellion and rebuilding | Includes glossary and index.
Identifiers: LCCN ISBN 9781538340820 (pbk.) | ISBN 9781538340813 (library bound) |
ISBN 9781538340837 (6 pack)
Subjects: LCSH: Gettysburg, Battle of, Gettysburg, Pa., 1863--Juvenile literature.
Classification: LCC E475.53 B388 2018 | DDC 973.7'349--dc23

Designer: Katelyn E. Reynolds
Editor: Joanne Randolph

Photo credits: Cvr, p. 1 Stock Montage/Getty Images; cvr, pp. 1–32 (background texture)
javarman/Shutterstock.com; cvr, pp. 1–32 (flags) cybrain/Shutterstock.com; cvr, pp. 1–32
(scroll) Seregam/Shutterstock.com; p. 5 National Archives and Records Administration,
cataloged under the National Archives Identifier (NAID) 528293 (https://catalog.archives.
gov/id/528293)/Wikipedia.org; p. 6 Júlio Reis/Tintazul/Wikipedia.org; p. 8 The Library of
Congress Prints & Photographs Online Catalog/Wikipedia.org; p. 11 De Agostini Picture
Library/Getty Images; pp. 12–15, 19–20, 24, 28 courtesy of the Library of Congress; p. 16
Zack Frank/Shutterstock.com; p. 22 Globe Turner/Shutterstock.com; p. 26 Map by Hal
Jespersen, www.posix.com/CW/Hlj/Wikipedia.org.

Manufactured in the United States of America

CPSIA Compliance Information: Batch #CS18PK: For Further Information contact Rosen Publishing, New York, New York at 1-800-237-9932

CONTENTS

WORDS IN THE GLOSSARY APPEAR
IN **BOLD** TYPE THE FIRST TIME
THEY ARE USED IN THE TEXT.

★

GETTYSBURG AND THE CIVIL WAR

President-elect Abraham Lincoln was worried as he prepared to take office as the 16th president of the United States on March 4, 1861. Seven southern states refused to accept Lincoln as their president and they had **seceded** from the Union. They had elected Jefferson Davis as president of their newly formed nation called the Confederate States of America. And four more slaveholding states were prepared to join their southern neighbors.

Two presidents. Two constitutions. Two nations, each insisting on their own **sovereignty**. Was it lawful for states to withdraw from the Union? Was the U.S. Constitution only a compact that a handful of states could choose to dissolve? For years these questions had been debated, but without resolution. The North and the South had grown apart, developing different ways of life with different kinds of problems. States' rights, the future of slavery, industrial versus agricultural interests — the two regions could not agree on any of these major issues.

Jefferson Davis, shown here, served as President of the Confederate States from 1861 to 1865.

★

5

THIS MAP SHOWS THE DIVISION OF STATES
AND TERRITORIES IN 1864,
WELL INTO THE AMERICAN CIVIL WAR.

★

UNION STATES

UNION STATES THAT PERMITTED SLAVERY

CONFEDERATE STATES

TERRITORIES

Confrontation between the North and the South seemed unavoidable. On April 17, 1861, hostilities began when the Confederates attacked Fort Sumter at Charleston, South Carolina.

Few people believed that the war would last very long — maybe three months at the longest. But each side underestimated the other, and the war lasted four long years.

To many historians, the war's most **pivotal** battle took place during the first three days of July in 1863. That's when circumstances brought the Union and Confederates armies together at a small Pennsylvania farm community known as Gettysburg.

When small advance units for both armies clashed around Gettysburg on July 1, the two opposing armies converged on the site. On the second day of fighting, after attacking both Union **flanks**, Confederate forces failed to push the Union army from its strong defensive position.

Confederate general Robert E. Lee might have retreated that afternoon, but instead he ordered a massive attack for the following day, July 3, 1863. He hoped to defeat the Union army once and for all in this battle.

8

It was the most controversial decision of Lee's career. Major General George E. Pickett led a 12,000-man assault against the Union army. Pickett's Charge ended in a huge death toll and defeat for the South. Lee marched his beaten army south, never to invade the North again. For the Union army, it was more than a much-needed win. It made the Union generals realize that Lee was not **invincible**.

The Battle of Gettysburg has become known as the high-water mark of the Confederacy. The South never regained the glory and success it achieved in 1863.

Meanwhile, the Union army figured out how to use its superior numbers and better-equipped army to wear down the enemy. Finally, on April 9, 1865, Lee surrendered at Appomattox Court House in Virginia to end the war.

Even when the fighting stopped, the war's impact on the nation did not. One soldier out of every five who took part was killed in battle or died in camp. And while the question of whether or not it was lawful for a state to secede from the Union was resolved by the war and the practice of slavery was **abolished**, new questions arose. What role was the South going to play in the nation's future? How were the newly freed slaves going to be integrated into society? Answering these questions became much more complicated when President Abraham Lincoln was assassinated on April 14, just five days after Lee's surrender. It would take many years to rebuild the tattered nation.

GETTYSBURG: FROM FARMLAND TO BATTLEFIELD

Throughout the month of June 1863, thousands of Civil War soldiers marched north from Virginia to Pennsylvania. Dressed in blue, gray, and even homespun brown uniforms, they trekked 20 to 30 miles a day through the scorching heat. Hiking for hours over dusty, unpaved roads, the soldiers stopped for infrequent meals of pork and dry biscuits. Where were they heading at such speed? To the next battle in the Civil War. And where would it take place? No one knew.

Still they struggled on, many dying of sunstroke under the hot June sun. Although they did not know it, they were converging on Gettysburg, Pennsylvania, destined to become one of the bloodiest battlegrounds of the war. In its 25-square-mile area, 160,000 Americans would fight during the first three days of July 1863. Of those, 50,000 would be wounded, captured, or killed.

What drew them to Gettysburg? This quiet Pennsylvania farm town lay 70 miles northwest of Washington, D.C., and was located at the intersection of nine major roads. Confederate general Robert E. Lee planned to invade the north; Union general George Meade intended to make his stand in Maryland. When Union and Confederate soldiers clashed near Gettysburg, coincidence, not strategy, brought them together.

THIS PAINTING SHOWS
GENERAL ROBERT E. LEE ON HORSEBACK,
SALUTING HIS TROOPS
AS THEY HEAD TO THE BATTLEFRONT.

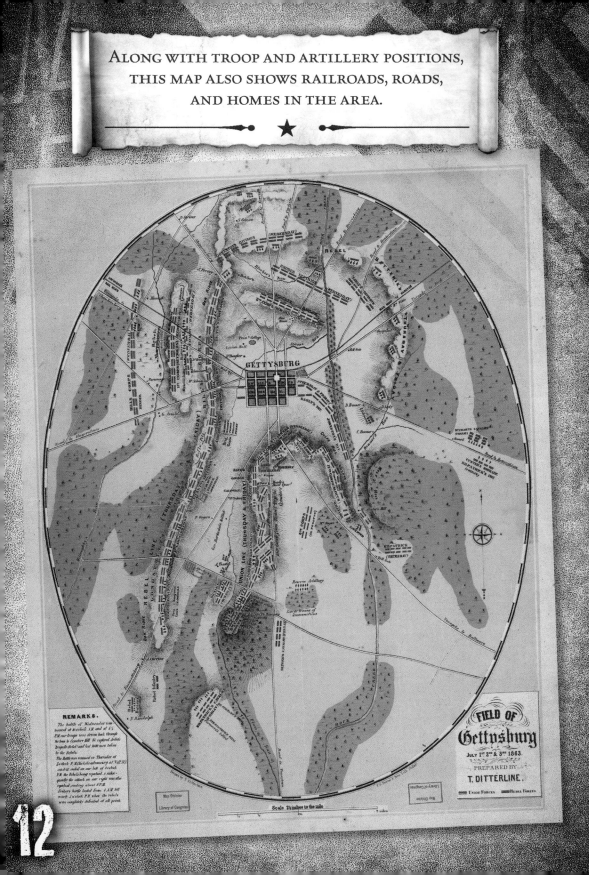

What did Gettysburg look like in 1863? This was farm country, with rural roads, split-rail and stone fences, barns, and log, frame, stone, and brick houses. Bluebells and hollyhocks bloomed abundantly in the gardens, and the fertile land supported corn, wheat, and peach and apple orchards.

Founded in 1786, the town was named for James Gettys, who had laid out 210 lots on his father's old farm. By the Civil War, Gettysburg was home to more than 2,000 **inhabitants**. Located in a prosperous market region, it featured two colleges, the Lutheran Theological Seminary, high on Seminary Ridge, and Pennsylvania College.

Gettysburg was set amid rolling hills, ridges, and valleys. Seminary Ridge lay to the west and Culp's Hill to the southeast. Cemetery Hill and Little and Big Round Tops framed the shallow valley, which measured 2 miles from north to south and half a mile wide. It was an ideal spot for nineteenth-century warfare, which focused on strategic heights and maneuvers.

LITTLE ROUND TOP

This photograph, taken in August 1863, shows the tents comprising General Hospital in Gettysburg, where many of the wounded were cared for.

When the two armies met, they fought in a wheat field and a peach orchard, where the fruit was just beginning to ripen. They also fought in Devil's Den amid a jumble of rocks and trees. Bullets passed within inches of homes, and many **civilians** fled their burning farms. The remains of the thousands of soldiers who died littered the fields and yards, and the town's colleges, churches, and homes, as well as surrounding farmsteads, were converted into hospitals for the wounded.

Gettysburg's citizens suffered, too. Houses were occupied by Confederate troops, and one civilian, Jennie Wade, was killed while caring for her sister and her sister's newborn child near Cemetery Hill. A Confederate bullet pierced two doors of the house she was in and struck her while she was baking bread.

Schoolteacher J. Howard Wert was able to collect battle **souvenirs**—a fife, shaving mirror, drum ornament, and blanket **insignia**—within yards of his family home. Other families also retrieved battle relics, and many solid-shot cannonballs became doorstops and paperweights.

DEVIL'S DEN

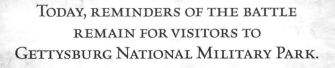

When the battle ended, artists and photographers descended on Gettysburg. Alexander Gardner rumbled into town with two horse-drawn darkrooms and began recording the scene. By the time Mathew Brady arrived, the dead had been buried, so he **documented** the landscape, taking panoramic shots of Little Round Top and Cemetery Hill. In 1866, after the Civil War had concluded, artist Peter Frederick Rothermel tramped the fields with former soldiers. He sketched faces and locations, then created a series of paintings immortalizing the battlefield.

The town of Gettysburg also had changed. Bullet holes scarred the trees, farm fields had been ruined, and lives had been torn apart, as the quiet village had been transformed into a battleground.

Today, the 3,500-acre Gettysburg National Military Park surrounds the town itself. Seminary Ridge, Culp's Hill, Little and Big Round Tops, Devil's Den, Cemetery Hill, Wheat Field, and Peach Orchard are all located within the park's borders. The 17-acre national cemetery contains more than 3,500 graves of Union soldiers who died at Gettysburg. Thirty miles of roads wind through the park, battlefield guides lead informational tours, and a 75-foot observation tower offers extraordinary views of the site. A visitor center features displays, while more than a thousand markers and monuments highlight significant battlefield locations. Gettysburg is every inch a Civil War site. It is hard to believe that the town was once just a peaceful farm community in the Pennsylvania countryside.

LOST AT GETTYSBURG

On May 14, 1863, a gray-bearded soldier rode the train to Richmond, Virginia. As the train clattered along the tracks, the soldier watched the greening countryside and thought about plans for a possible **campaign**. This soldier, General Robert E. Lee, was the commander of Confederate troops in the East. He was going to Richmond to meet with the president of the Confederacy, Jefferson Davis.

General Lee looked pale, thin, and worried. He fretted because Union troops under General Ulysses S. Grant had surrounded Vicksburg, a southern fortress that protected the Mississippi River. Grant's troops had stopped the flow of much-needed supplies to the Confederate soldiers there. Other Union troops under General Joseph Hooker threatened Richmond, the capital of the South. General Lee agonized over his plan to turn the Civil War in the South's favor.

In this image, Robert E. Lee (right) appears to be discussing battle tactics with Jefferson Davis (left).

★

19

GENERAL JOSEPH HOOKER, SHOWN HERE,
WAS GIVEN THE NICKNAME
"FIGHTING JOE."

In Richmond, Lee met with Davis and explained his plan. The general felt that the South must make a major offensive into Union territory. He hoped this offensive would take the pressure off Richmond, disrupt Federal railroads, get supplies for his troops, and encourage European countries to send a fleet in support of the Confederacy. President Davis approved Lee's plan and sent him back to his men.

A few days later, Lee started his army northward, a move that surprised many Union officers. They could not believe that Lee would leave Richmond and head into enemy territory. The Union army followed the Confederate troops, while the Union **cavalry** mounted attacks on the Southerners. But Lee and his army marched on.

General Hooker, commander of the Union army, responded cautiously. Hooker had lost one battle to Lee at Chancellorsville, Virginia, and he did not want to lose another. He allowed the Confederates to advance uncontested, and the South gradually gained the momentum that Lee had hoped for. One Confederate soldier wrote in his diary that in a single day he had consumed "breakfast in Virginia, whiskey in Maryland, and supper in Pennsylvania." As the Confederate troops advanced, they defeated a Union force at Winchester, Virginia, and secured the supplies they needed to continue.

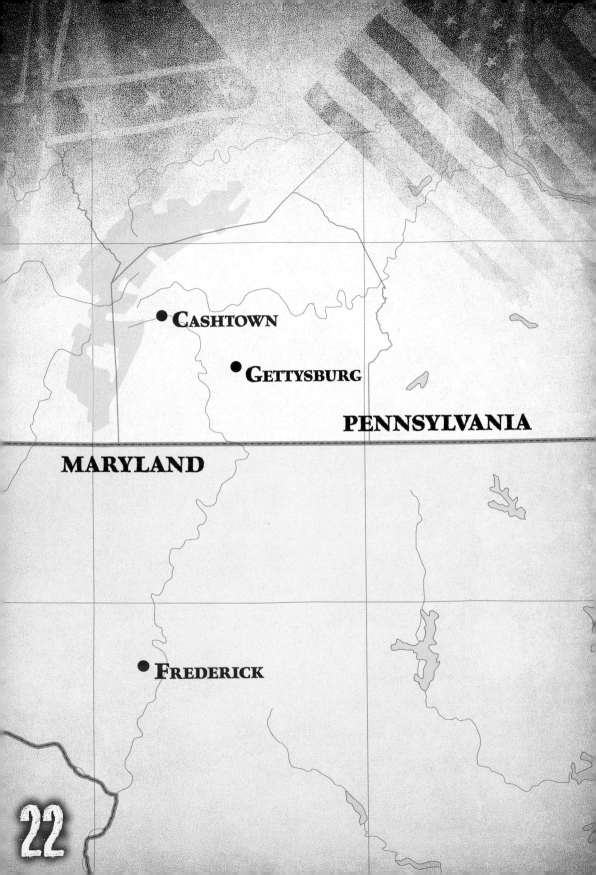

CASHTOWN

GETTYSBURG

PENNSYLVANIA

MARYLAND

FREDERICK

In reality, Lee had fewer soldiers than the Union army, and his men were poorly equipped. The Union officers, President Lincoln, and the people of the North overestimated Lee's strength. However, fearing an attack, civilians fled to safety, and shopkeepers shipped the goods from their stores to towns farther away.

President Lincoln especially worried about the safety of Washington, D.C., and Baltimore. Near the end of the march, Lee's cavalry somehow ended up on the other side of the enemy's lines. In those days, the horse-mounted cavalry served as the "eyes and ears of the army." Therefore, Lee was forced to continue north without knowing the exact position of the Union troops. On June 28, a Confederate spy reported to Lee that he saw Union troops camped a few miles east in Frederick, Maryland. Shocked, Lee ordered his troops to come together in Cashtown, Pennsylvania, with the mountains at their back to protect their flanks and rear.

While Lee moved north, Lincoln pondered the situation. General Hooker had lost the confidence of the government and the nation. Thus, Lincoln decided to replace him with General George Meade. Meade was not well known to the nation, but he was a reliable officer and had performed well in other battles.

General George G. Meade, shown here, led Union forces to a victory at Gettysburg, although the loss of life on both sides of the battle was devastating.

Both Meade and Lee knew that they would soon face each other in battle. Meade pushed his army north from Frederick, always conscious that he must protect Washington and Baltimore, while Lee's army stayed at Cashtown. On July 1, one of the Confederate generals sent men to Gettysburg to find supplies and shoes for the Southern soldiers. Meade had cavalry there to resist a Confederate advance.

Almost accidentally, a battle broke out between divisions of the Southern and Northern armies. Lee and Meade kept sending more men into the fight, and soon both armies were heavily engaged. Union troops originally fought north and west of Gettysburg, but Lee's troops pushed the Union back to a ridge running south of town. The Southerners had the momentum, and it appeared by the end of the first day of fighting that they would win.

July 2 dawned hot and sultry. General Lee rose at 3:30 a.m. to plan the day's battle. Later that morning, he and his commanding officers charted their attack on Meade. They decided that a large force of Confederates who had arrived during the night would attack the southern flank of the Union army while other Southern forces attacked the right flank. They hoped to strike the Union army with a surprisingly strong blow at a weak point.

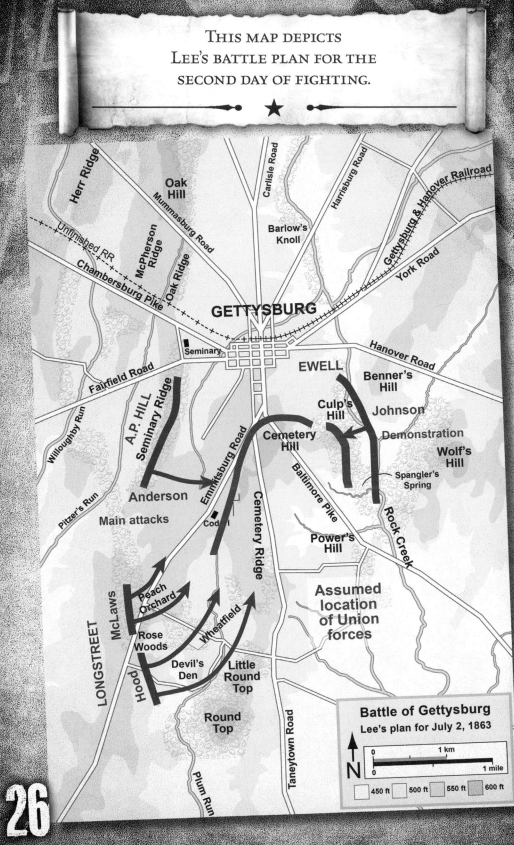

THIS MAP DEPICTS LEE'S BATTLE PLAN FOR THE SECOND DAY OF FIGHTING.

Reportedly, one of Lee's officers, General Longstreet, felt uneasy about the battle plan. He feared that the Union troops held too many strong positions on the battlefield. Thus, he slowly and reluctantly moved his troops into position. Precious time slipped away as the commanding officers readied for battle.

Meanwhile, more Union soldiers arrived, and on the right flank they built walls of stone and logs for protection. Finally, at four that afternoon, the battle started. Time after time, the Confederates attacked the Union positions. But the Union lines held, and by nightfall the Confederate troops had lost many men and gained little ground.

The next day Lee tried once again to destroy the Union army. Confederate cannons fired on the enemy, but the Union soldiers laid low behind rocks and rails. Consequently, the Confederate cannon fire caused few injuries. Then the Union troops opened up with their own cannons. For more than an hour, the cannons blasted away at each other. Union officers watching the battle finally decided to stop firing their cannons and save ammunition.

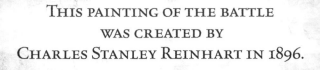

The Confederate officers concluded that their cannons had destroyed several Union strongholds. Therefore, the officers ordered 12,000 of their soldiers to attack the middle of Meade's defensive line. As the Confederate army moved forward, Union soldiers opened up with cannon fire and guns.

Confederate soldiers fell by the thousands. Only a few hundred reached the ridge, where many fell to Union **bayonets**. Others were taken prisoner.

The offensive had failed, and the Confederates had lost their momentum. About 3,000 Confederate soldiers lay dead as a result of 3 days of hard fighting. Many more would die from wounds or disease. Devastated by the defeat, Lee and his troops retreated south.

Historians call Gettysburg the high-water mark of the Civil War because the South would never again strongly advance so far into the North. Lee had lost thousands of fighting men, and his troops had consumed many badly needed supplies. The South had lost its momentum and all hope of obtaining European support. Two years later, General Robert E. Lee surrendered his army to General Ulysses S. Grant at Appomattox, Virginia, but in many people's minds, the war had been lost at Gettysburg.

GLOSSARY

abolished: Did away with something believed to be harmful to society, such as slavery.

bayonets: Sword-like, stabbing blades affixed to the ends of guns to be used when hand-to-hand combat was needed.

campaign: A series of military actions that are designed to achieve a certain purpose, usually in a certain area or using a particular kind of fighting.

cavalry: Soldiers who fight on horseback.

civilians: People who are not part of the military or police force.

document: To record something through writing or images.

flanks: The right or left side of a large body of people, such as a military unit.

inhabitants: The people who live in a particular place.

insignia: A badge or mark showing a military rank, office, or membership in an organization.

invincible: Unbeatable.

pivotal: Crucial to the success of something.

seceded: Withdrew formally from a federal, political, or religious alliance.

souvenirs: Things that are kept as a reminder of a person, place, or particular event.

sovereignty: The authority of a state or body to govern itself or another state or body.

FOR MORE INFORMATION

BOOKS

Johnson, Jennifer. *Gettysburg: The Bloodiest Battle of the War*. London: Franklin Watts Press, 2009.

Martin, Iain C. *Gettysburg: The True Account of Two Young Heroes in the Greatest Battle of the Civil War*. New York: Sky Pony Press, 2015.

WEBSITES

Gettysburg
https://www.civilwar.org/learn/civil-war/battles/gettysburg

Battle of Gettysburg
http://www.history.com/topics/american-civil-war/battle-of-gettysburg

INDEX